I0818559

ARMED FORCES OF THE UNITED STATES

THE UNITED STATES AIR FORCE

TORQUE™

BY DONNA MCKINNEY

BELLWETHER MEDIA • MINNEAPOLIS, MN

Torque brims with excitement perfect for thrill-seekers of all kinds. Discover daring survival skills, explore uncharted worlds, and marvel at mighty engines and extreme sports. In *Torque* books, anything can happen. Are you ready?

This edition first published in 2025 by Bellwether Media, Inc.

Library of Congress Cataloging-in-Publication Data

Names: McKinney, Donna B. (Donna Bowen), author.
Title: The United States Air Force / by Donna McKinney.
Description: Minneapolis, MN : Bellwether Media, Inc., 2025. | Series: Torque : Armed forces of the United States | Includes bibliographical references and index. | Audience: Ages 7-12 | Audience: Grades 4-6 |
Summary: "Engaging images accompany information about the United States Air Force. The combination of high-interest subject matter and light text is intended for students in grades 3 through 7"– Provided by publisher.
Identifiers: LCCN 2024016013 (print) | LCCN 2024016014 (ebook) | ISBN 9798893040104 (library binding) | ISBN 9781644879429 (ebook)
Subjects: LCSH: United States. Air Force–Juvenile literature.
Classification: LCC UG633 .M235 2025 (print) | LCC UG633 (ebook) | DDC 358.400973–dc23/eng/20240411
LC record available at https://lccn.loc.gov/2024016013
LC ebook record available at https://lccn.loc.gov/2024016014

Editor: Rebecca Sabelko Designer: Jeffrey Kollock

Printed in the United States of America, North Mankato, MN.

TABLE OF CONTENTS

HELP IN A DISASTER

EARTHQUAKE DAMAGE

It is August 16, 2021. People in Haiti need help! A major **earthquake** has left many hurt. They also need supplies. The United States Air Force is called to action!

Airmen quickly arrive in Haiti. They set up a landing area for supply airplanes. They help the airplanes safely land. People in Haiti get supplies they need.

DEFENDING THE AIR

The Air Force carries out U.S. military **missions** in the air. People who serve are called Airmen. Airmen mostly work with airplanes and helicopters. Some Airmen fly aircraft. Others have flight support jobs.

The **Pentagon** is the Air Force **headquarters**. Air Force **bases** are in the U.S., Europe, and Asia.

AIR FORCE ACADEMY

The Air Force Academy is near Colorado Springs, Colorado. Students become Air Force officers when they finish school.

AIRMEN
BASE
PENTAGON

Airmen fight enemies in the air during times of war. They also fight on the ground and on water. Airmen **scout** enemies. They move troops and supplies.

Airmen build airstrips during peacetime. They train for war. They guard U.S. **missile** sites. They rescue people and bring supplies when disasters happen. The Air Force also studies ways to improve weapons and aircraft.

AIR FORCE BASES

AIR FORCE AIRCRAFT AND WEAPONS

UNITED STATES AIR FORCE

F-16 FIGHTING FALCON

Airmen fly many kinds of aircraft. They fly **combat** fighters like F-16 Fighting Falcons. B-2 Spirits are **stealth** bombers.

MQ-9 REAPER

CV-22 Ospreys take off and land like helicopters. But they fly fast like airplanes. Ospreys carry troops and supplies. MQ-9 Reapers are **drones** controlled from the ground. They carry weapons. They also look for enemies and help with rescues.

Aircraft carry weapons like cannons, missiles, and bombs. A-10 Thunderbolt IIs are armed with GAU-8 Avengers. These cannons are called tank busters. They have a lot of power!

F-15 Eagles and F-16 Fighting Falcons carry powerful missiles. AIM-7M Sparrows are missiles guided by **radar**. AIM-9 Sidewinders can travel faster than the speed of sound.

MISSIONS

Airmen complete many important missions. People in Berlin, Germany, needed food and other supplies in 1948. But **Soviet** troops blocked ground delivery efforts.

Airmen carried out the Berlin Airlift mission. They flew supplies into Berlin. Each airplane carried up to 10 tons (9 metric tons) of supplies. The Air Force made over 189,000 flights.

SOVIET TROOPS

THE AIR TRANSPORT COMMAND
BERLIN AIRLIFT MISSION
SUPPLIES

ATTACK ON AN IRAQI OIL FIELD DURING OPERATION DESERT STRIKE

Iraqi troops attacked the Kurdish people in Iraq in 1996. The Air Force fought back with Operation Desert Strike. Airmen flew B-52 bombers to fight Iraqi troops.

B-52s are long-range heavy bombers. The bombers flew 34 hours non-stop. It was the longest bombing mission in history.

B-52 BOMBER

INSIDE A B-52

Terrorists attacked the U.S. on September 11, 2001. The military started Operation Noble Eagle. Thousands of Airmen kept watch over major cities.

OPERATION NOBLE EAGLE

SEPTEMBER 11, 2001, ATTACK

The Air Force used many airplanes for Operation Noble Eagle. Fighter jets, **tankers**, and early warning airplanes were part of the job. The Air Force works to keep the country safe.

MISSION

WILDFIRES IN NORTHERN CALIFORNIA

YEAR 2017

PURPOSE

AIR FORCE AIRMEN PILOTED THE MQ-9 REAPER DRONE OVER A MASSIVE WILDFIRE IN CALIFORNIA

RESULTS

THE REAPER GAVE FIREFIGHTERS REAL-TIME IMAGES OF THE FIRE

AIR FORCE PROFILE

MEMBERS TO REMEMBER

LIEUTENANT GENERAL SUSAN HELMS
An Air Force officer and NASA astronaut who was the first U.S. military woman in space

GENERAL DANIEL "CHAPPIE" JAMES JR.
The first Black man to become a 4-star general in any U.S. military branch

GENERAL CHARLES YEAGER
The first human to fly faster than the speed of sound

MISSIONS

CUBAN MISSILE CRISIS
1962

OPERATION IRAQI FREEDOM
2003

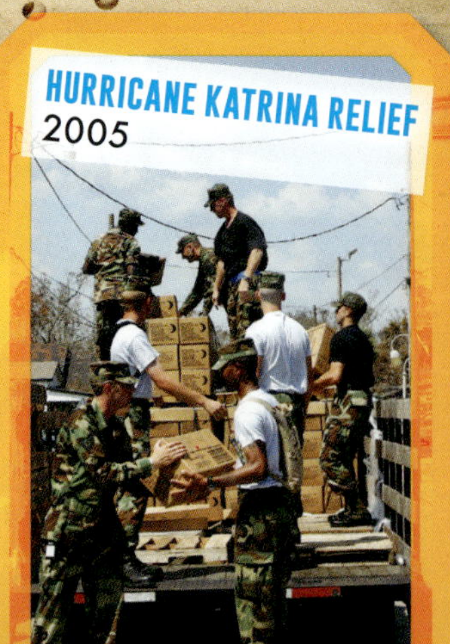

HURRICANE KATRINA RELIEF
2005

EMBLEM

LOGO

MOTTO "Aim High ... Fly-Fight-Win"

YEAR ESTABLISHED 1947

NUMBER OF MEMBERS

active duty in 2023
323,400

RANKS

Airman

General

GLOSSARY

bases—places where armed forces train and work

combat—related to a fight between armed forces

drones—aircraft that are flown by a remote control or by computers

earthquake—an event in which the earth's surface shakes; earthquakes often cause a lot of damage.

headquarters—the main office of an organization

missile—a weapon that travels in the air and explodes when it hits a target

missions—jobs that Air Force headquarters assigns to Airmen

Pentagon—a building in Arlington, Virginia, that is headquarters for the U.S. military

radar—a device or system that sends out radio waves to find objects

scout—to look for and track an enemy's position

Soviet—a country in eastern Europe and northern Asia from 1922 to 1991

stealth—related to technology used to hide aircraft or vehicles from radar

tankers—airplanes that carry fuel to refuel other aircraft in the air

terrorists—people who use fear to control others

TO LEARN MORE

AT THE LIBRARY

Billings, Tanner. *The U.S. Air Force.* New York, N.Y.: Rosen Publishing, 2022.

McKinney, Donna. *B-2 Stealth Bomber.* Minneapolis, Minn.: Bellwether Media, 2024.

Ringstad, Arnold. *US Air Force: Equipment and Vehicles.* Minneapolis, Minn.: Abdo Publishing, 2022.

ON THE WEB

FACTSURFER

Factsurfer.com gives you a safe, fun way to find more information.

1. Go to www.factsurfer.com
2. Enter "The United States Air Force" into the search box and click 🔍.
3. Select your book cover to see a list of related content.

INDEX

The images in this book are reproduced through the courtesy of: US Navy, front cover; NA, p. 3; Associated Press/ AP Images, p. 4; USAF, pp. 5, 9 (San Antonio), 17 (inside); DVIDS, pp. 5 (inset), 6, 7 (Airmen, base), 8 (main, inset), 9 (Eglin), 10, 11 (main, B-2 Spirit), 12 (main, inset), 13, 16 (fun fact), 17 (B-52), 20 (Cuban Missile Crisis), 23; Jeremy Christensen, p. 7 (Pentagon); Andrew Britten/ Wikipedia Commons, p. 9 (Elmendorf-Richardson); Thomas Barrat, p. 9 (MacDill); Derek Beattie Images, p. 13 (fun fact); SuperStock/ Alamy, p. 14; Department of Defense, p. 15 (top); Everett Collection Historical/ Alamy, p. 15 (middle); CBW/ Alamy, p. 15 (bottom); NB/ROD/ Alamy, p. 16; USAF/ Wikipedia Commons, pp. 18, 20 (Helms, James), 21 (emblem, logo, Airmen, General); rds323/ Wikipedia Commons, p. 18 (inset); NASA/ Wikpedia Commons, p. 19 (left); Elliott Cowand Jr, p. 19 (right); Jason Edwards/ Wikipedia Commons, p. 20 (Yeager); USAF/ Alamy, p. 20 (Iraqi Freedom); Wirestock Creators, p. 20 (Hurricane Katrina).